THE PLANETS IN OUR SOLAR SYSTEM

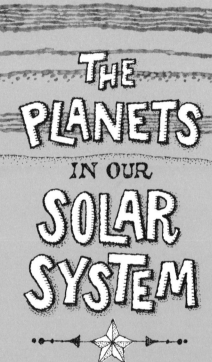

# THE PLANETS IN OUR SOLAR SYSTEM

Franklyn M. Branley
Illustrated by Don Madden

Thomas Y. Crowell    New York

OTHER *Let's-Read-and-Find-Out Science Books* YOU WILL ENJOY

*The Big Dipper* by Franklyn M. Branley · *Energy from the Sun* by Melvin Berger · *Eclipse* by Franklyn M. Branley · *The Moon Seems to Change* by Franklyn M. Branley · *The Sun* by Franklyn M. Branley · *Sunshine Makes the Seasons* by Franklyn M. Branley · *What Makes Day and Night* by Franklyn M. Branley

*Let's-Read-and-Find-Out Science Books* are edited by Dr. Roma Gans, Professor Emeritus of Childhood Education, Teachers College, Columbia University, and by Dr. Franklyn M. Branley, Astronomer Emeritus and former Chairman of The American Museum–Hayden Planetarium. For a complete catalog of *Let's-Read-and-Find-Out Science Books,* write to Thomas Y. Crowell, Department 363, 10 East 53rd Street, New York, New York 10022.

Grateful acknowledgment is made to the Jet Propulsion Laboratory for the photographs of Mercury on page 2 and Mars and Jupiter on page 3; the National Aeronautics and Space Administration for the photographs of Earth, Saturn and Venus on page 3 and Comet West on page 11; Mount Wilson and Las Campanas Observatories, Carnegie Institution of Washington for the photograph of the moon on page 8; and the Hansen Planetarium for the photograph of the meteoroid on page 11.

*Library of Congress Cataloging in Publication Data*
Branley, Franklyn Mansfield, 1915–    The planets in our solar system. (Let's-read-and-find-out science book)
SUMMARY: Introduces the solar system and its nine planets. Includes directions for making two models: one showing relative sizes of the planets, and the other, their relative distances from the sun. 1. Planets—Juvenile literature. [1. Planets. 2. Solar system] I. Madden, Don, 1927–   II. Title.
QB602.B73   1981   523.4   79-7894   ISBN 0-690-04025-3   ISBN 0-690-04026-1 (lib. bdg.)

We all live on a planet. Our planet is called Earth. It is one of nine planets that go around the sun.

You probably know the names of some of the planets. Maybe you know all of them. The nine planets are Mercury, Venus, Earth, Mars, Jupiter, Saturn, Uranus, Neptune, and Pluto.

The nine planets are parts of the solar system.

Surface of Mercury

These photographs show six of the planets in our solar system. We don't yet have good close-up photographs of the others.

Saturn

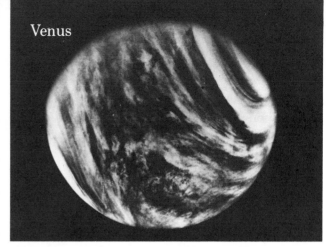

Venus

Earth

Jupiter

Mars

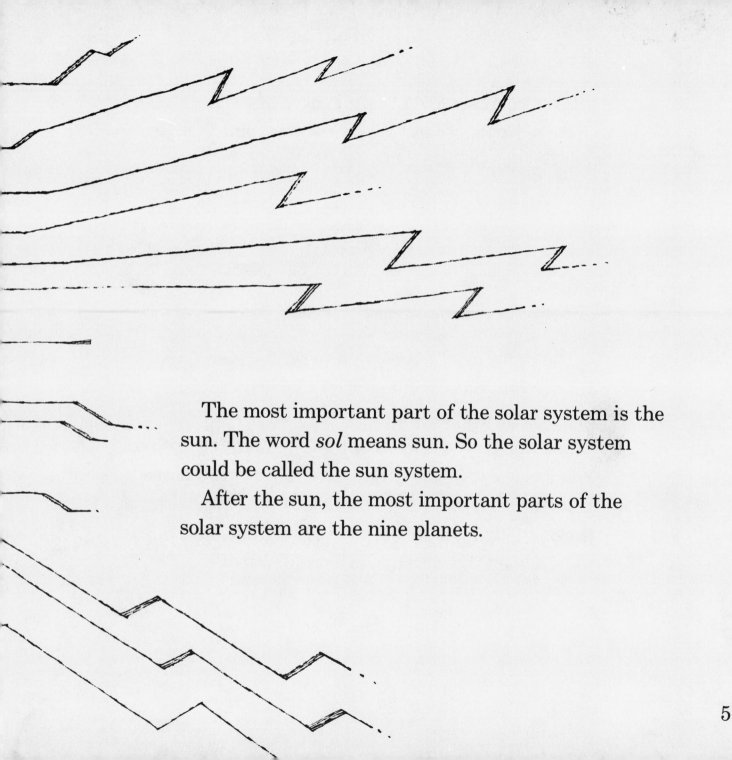

The most important part of the solar system is the sun. The word *sol* means sun. So the solar system could be called the sun system.

After the sun, the most important parts of the solar system are the nine planets.

Have you ever tried to find the planets in the sky? Uranus, Neptune, and Pluto are very dim. You would need a telescope to see them.

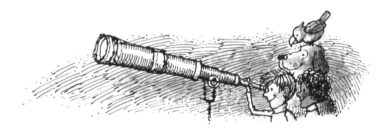

You don't need a telescope to see Venus, Mars, Jupiter, and Saturn. They look like bright stars. You may have seen them and thought they were stars.

You don't need a telescope to see Mercury, either. You can see it in the early evening just after sunset, or in the early morning just before sunrise. At these times, though, the sky is not very dark. You'll have to be a good sky-watcher to find Mercury.

The moon

But there is another part of the solar system that you can easily see. It is the moon.

The moon does not go around the sun. It goes around the Earth. It is sometimes called Earth's satellite.

Most of the other planets have satellites, too. But you would need a telescope to see them.

Earth

Moon

The moon goes around Earth.

Asteroids are also part of the solar system. So are comets and meteoroids. Asteroids are big chunks of rock that go around the sun. Many are as big as a house. Some are as big as a mountain, even bigger.

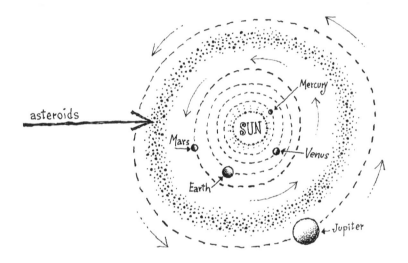

Comets are collections of ice, gas, and dust. They may be a thousand miles from one side to the other.

Meteoroids are bits of rock and metal. Some are large, but most are as small as grains of sand. Have you ever seen a shooting star? It was not really a star. It was a meteoroid falling toward Earth.

This is a photograph of a bright comet named Comet West, which is about 50 million miles long from head to tail.

The long streak in this photograph is the trail of a meteoroid falling toward Earth.

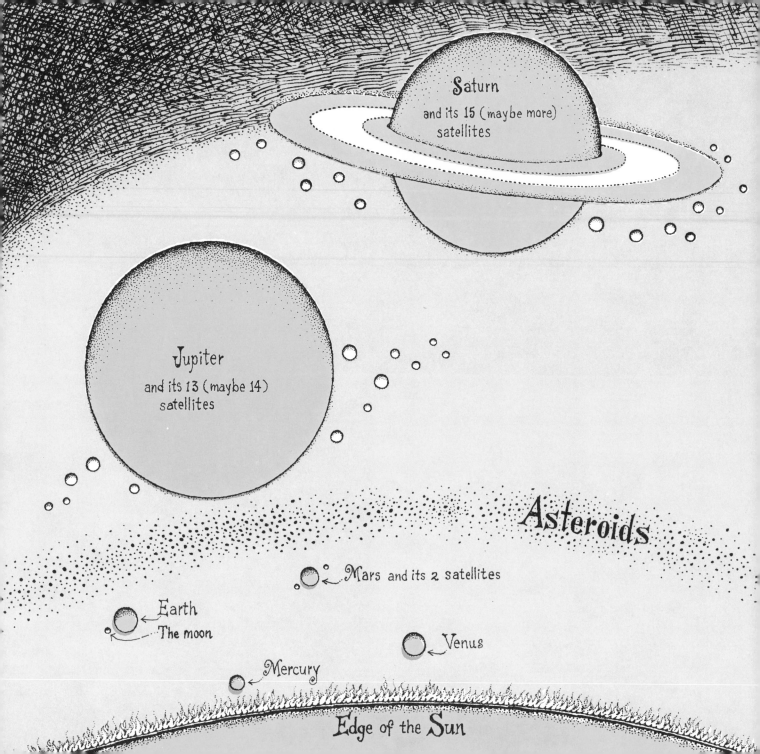

Uranus
and its 5
satellites

Pluto
and its satellite

Neptune
and its 2
satellites

The solar system has many parts—the sun, the nine planets, the satellites of the planets, asteroids, comets, and meteoroids. But the main parts are the sun and the nine planets.

Neptune

Pluto

The nine planets move around the sun. They move in paths called orbits. The drawing shows where the orbits are, but you can't really see orbits in space.

Mercury takes only 88 days to go around the sun once.

Pluto takes much longer than that. It takes about 248 years!

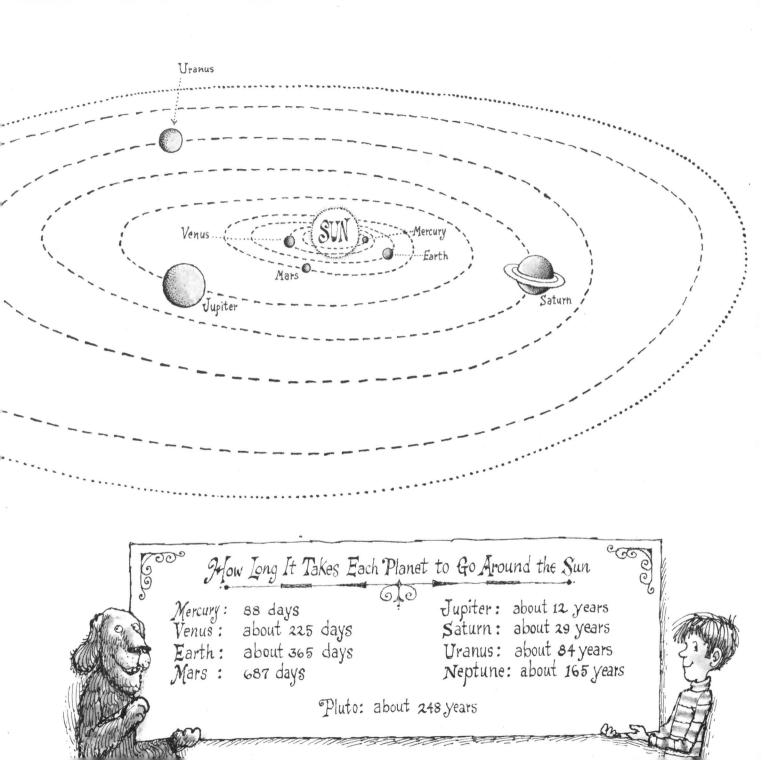

Uranus

Venus · · · · · Mercury

SUN

Earth

Mars

Jupiter

Saturn

## How Long It Takes Each Planet to Go Around the Sun

Mercury: 88 days
Venus: about 225 days
Earth: about 365 days
Mars: 687 days

Jupiter: about 12 years
Saturn: about 29 years
Uranus: about 84 years
Neptune: about 165 years

Pluto: about 248 years

Mercury is closer to the sun than any other plane, but even Mercury is millions of miles away from the sun.

Suppose you could fly from Mercury to the sun in a rocket. And suppose the rocket went 50,000 miles (about 80,000 kilometers) an hour. It would take more than four weeks to get there.

It would take over six years to get to Neptune.

The same rocket would take less than three minutes to fly from Chicago to Los Angeles.

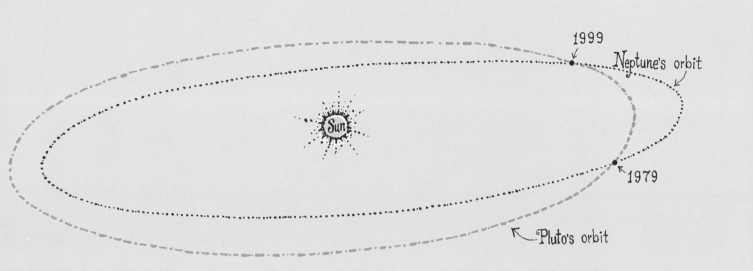

Neptune is farther from the sun than any other planet, but it wasn't always. Pluto was the farthest planet. Then in 1979, for the first time in hundreds of years, Pluto was a little closer to the sun than Neptune.

In 1999 Pluto will again become the farthest planet from the sun. How old will you be in 1999?

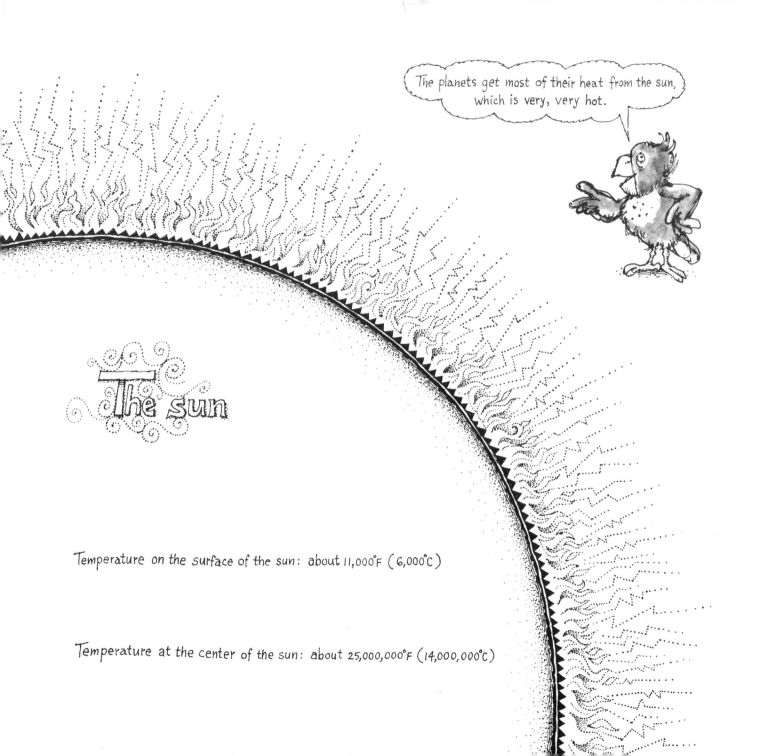

The planets get most of their heat from the sun, which is very, very hot.

# The sun

Temperature on the surface of the sun: about 11,000°F (6,000°C)

Temperature at the center of the sun: about 25,000,000°F (14,000,000°C)

Both Neptune and Pluto are far away from the sun. That is why they are the coldest planets. Temperatures there are about 328 degrees below zero Fahrenheit (200 degrees below zero Celsius).

That's much colder than any place on Earth. Even the South Pole never gets that cold.

Mercury and Venus are the hottest planets. Temperatures there are over 662 degrees Fahrenheit (350 degrees Celsius).

Plants and animals cannot live on Mercury or Venus. They would burn up. They cannot live on Neptune or Pluto either. They would freeze.

Of all the planets, Earth is the only one on which people live. In fact, we think no other planet in our solar system has plants or animals of any kind. Earth is the life planet.

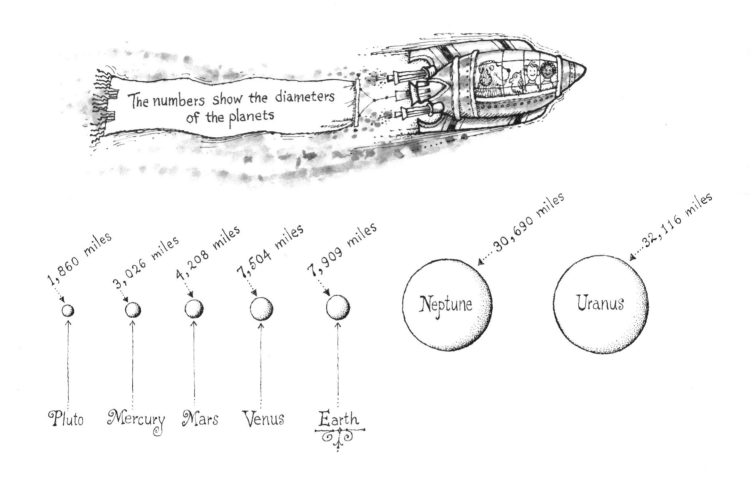

The numbers show the diameters of the planets

1,860 miles — Pluto
3,026 miles — Mercury
4,208 miles — Mars
7,504 miles — Venus
7,909 miles — Earth
30,690 miles — Neptune
32,116 miles — Uranus

Earth is a middle-sized planet. Four of the planets are smaller than Earth. They are Mercury, Venus, Mars, and Pluto. Four of the planets are larger than Earth. They are Jupiter, Saturn, Uranus, and Neptune.

Jupiter is the biggest of all the planets. It is much

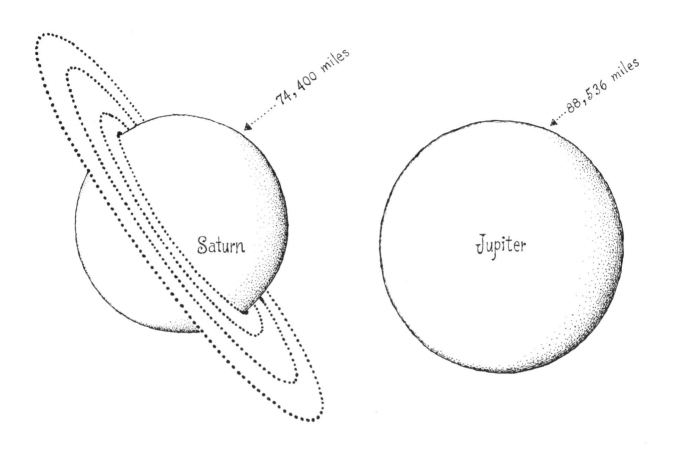

74,400 miles

Saturn

88,536 miles

Jupiter

bigger than Earth. Suppose Jupiter were a large,
hollow ball. Over 1,000 Earths could fit inside it.

Pluto is the smallest planet. It is much smaller
than Earth. More than 100,000 Plutos would fit
inside Jupiter.

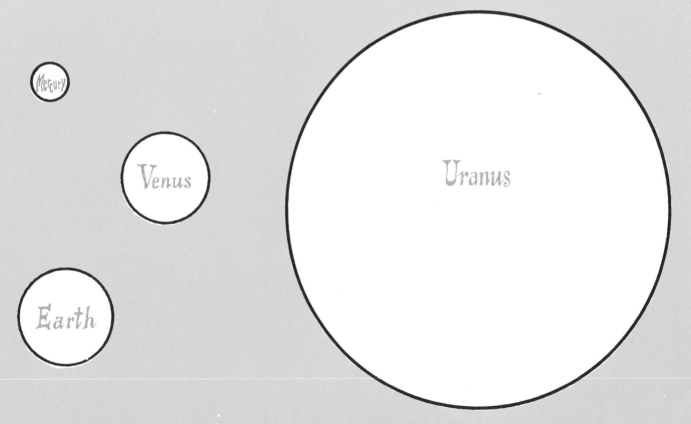

You can make a model of the solar system that will show the differences in the sizes of the planets.

You can use beads and balls for the planets. Or you can cut circles out of cardboard. That's what we did.

Trace the circles in the book. Jupiter and Saturn will be very large. We had enough space to show only a part of these two circles.

Here is an interesting project!

Mercury

Venus

Earth

Uranus

24

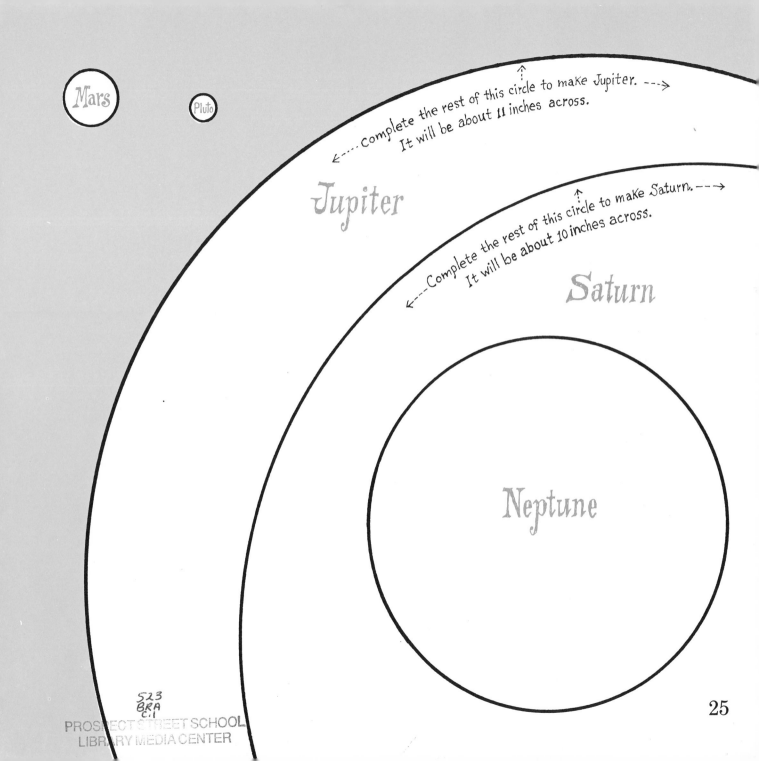

Mars

Pluto

←···· Complete the rest of this circle to make Jupiter. ---→
It will be about 11 inches across.

Jupiter

←--- Complete the rest of this circle to make Saturn. --→
It will be about 10 inches across.

Saturn

Neptune

25

1. After you have cut out the circles, tape or glue pieces of thread or light string to them. Make each string about 4 inches long.

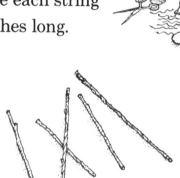

2. Gather five small twigs from bushes or trees. They don't have to be the same length. (Or you can use pieces of wire from coat hangers.)

3. Tie the string from Jupiter to one end of a twig.

4. Tie another planet—any one of them—to the other end of the twig. You can tape the strings in place if you want to.

5. Lay the twig across your finger. Move the twig from side to side until it balances. Mark that place. This is the balance point.

6. Tie a string around the mark. The planets should balance. If they don't, move the string until they do. Tape the string in place.

7. Fasten the other planets to twigs. Balance the twigs on your finger. Tie strings around the balance points.

8. One of the twigs will have only one planet, but that's all right. If the planet is a little one, the stick will still balance on your finger.

9. Tie each string from one twig to the balance point of another twig.

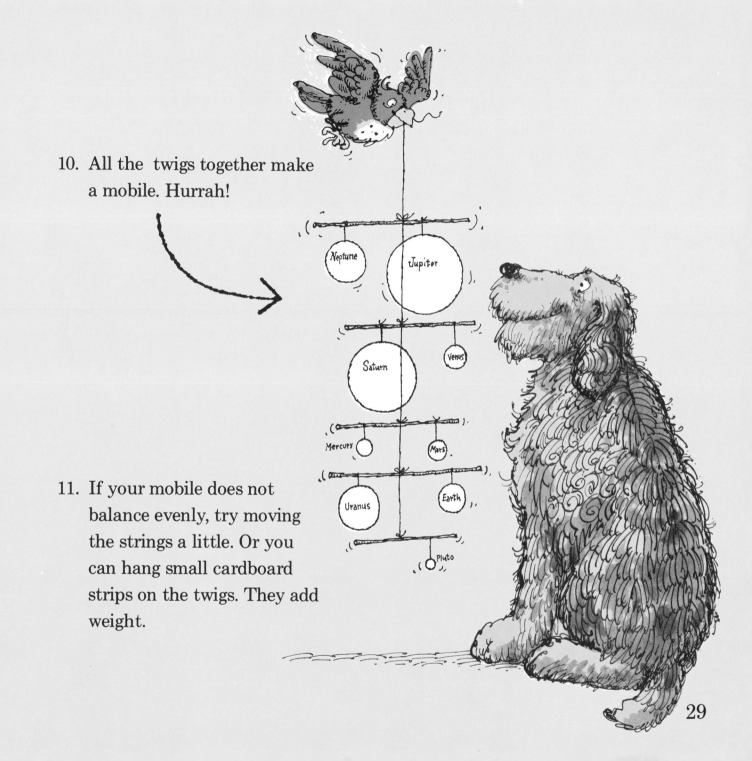

10. All the twigs together make
a mobile. Hurrah!

11. If your mobile does not
balance evenly, try moving
the strings a little. Or you
can hang small cardboard
strips on the twigs. They add
weight.

29

Here is another model you can make. This one shows the nine planets and the differences in their distance from the sun. To make this model, you'll need a long wall.

SUN

In this model each tack represents a planet. The names of the planets are on cardboard signs.

Mercury   Mars
Venus
Earth
Jupiter
Saturn
Uranus

Write the names of the planets on pieces of cardboard. The drawing shows how far from the sun each of the planets should be. Measure, then put the cardboard signs where they belong.

Hey! Look at me. I'm 2 billion, 788 million miles away!

Most of the time Pluto is farther from the sun than Neptune. That's why in our model we put Pluto here.

Neptune

Pluto

## DISTANCES OF THE PLANETS FROM THE SUN

MERCURY → 36 million miles (2 inches in your model)
VENUS → 67 million miles (3 inches in your model)
EARTH → 93 million miles (4 inches in your model)
MARS → 141 million miles (6 inches in your model)
JUPITER → 483 million miles (1 foot, 9 inches in your model)
SATURN → 885 million miles (3 feet, 2 inches in your model)
URANUS → 1 billion, 779 million miles (6 feet, 5 inches in your model)
NEPTUNE → 2 billion, 788 million miles (10 feet, 1 inch in your model)
PLUTO → 3 billion, 658 million miles (13 feet, 3 inches in your model)

Earth is the most important planet to you, and to all of us. That's because it's the planet on which we live. It is not the biggest planet in the solar system. Nor is it the smallest. It is not the hottest, nor the coldest. Earth is about in the middle. And it's just right for us.

| | Actual Diameter | | Diameter in Model | | Actual Mean Distance from Sun | | Distance in Model | |
|---|---|---|---|---|---|---|---|---|
| | Miles | Kilometers | Inches | Centimeters | Miles | Kilometers | Inches | Centimeters |
| Mercury | 3,026 | 4,880 | .39 | 1 | 35,898,000 | 57,900,000 | 1.56 | 4 |
| Venus | 7,504 | 12,104 | .97 | 2.48 | 67,084,000 | 108,200,000 | 2.91 | 7.48 |
| Earth | 7,909 | 12,756 | 1.02 | 2.61 | 92,752,000 | 149,600,000 | 4.03 | 10.34 |
| Mars | 4,208 | 6,787 | .54 | 1.39 | 141,298,000 | 227,900,000 | 6.14 | 15.74 |
| Jupiter | 88,536 | 142,800 | 11.41 | 29.26 | 482,546,000 | 778,300,000 | 20.97 | 53.77 |
| Saturn | 74,400 | 120,000 | 9.59 | 24.59 | 884,740,000 | 1,427,000,000 | 38.45 | 98.58 |
| Uranus | 32,116 | 51,800 | 4.14 | 10.61 | 1,779,152,000 | 2,869,600,000 | 77.31 | 198.25 |
| Neptune | 30,690 | 49,500 | 3.95 | 10.14 | 2,787,892,000 | 4,496,600,000 | 121.15 | 310.65 |
| Pluto | 1,860 | 3,000 | .24 | .61 | 3,658,000,000 | 5,900,000,000 | 158.96 | 407.60 |

In the directions for making the models, some sizes and distances are rounded to simplify the job of measuring. More exact sizes and distances are given above.